Prayer for My Enemy

T0155033

BOOKS BY CRAIG LUCAS AVAILABLE FROM TCG

The Light in the Piazza
Book by Craig Lucas
Music and Lyrics by Adam Guettel

Prayer for My Enemy

Prelude to a Kiss and Other Plays
ALSO INCLUDES:
Missing Persons
Three Postcards

Reckless and Other Plays
ALSO INCLUDES:
Blue Window
Stranger

What I Meant Was: New Plays and Selected One-Acts
ALSO INCLUDES:
The Dying Gaul
God's Heart

Prayer for My Enemy

A PLAY

Craig Lucas

THEATRE COMMUNICATIONS GROUP
NEW YORK
2009

Prayer for My Enemy is published by Theatre Communications Group, Inc.,
520 Eighth Avenue, 24th Floor, New York, NY 10018-4156

This publication is made possible in part with public funds from the New York State Council on the Arts, a State Agency.

TCG books are exclusively distributed to the book trade by Consortium Book Sales and Distribution.

LIBRARY OF CONGRESS CATALOGING-IN-PUBLICATION DATA

Lucas, Craig.
Prayer for my enemy : a play / Craig Lucas.
p. cm.
ISBN 978-1-55936-344-0
I. Title.
PS3562.U233P69 2009
812'.54—dc22   2009033299

Book design and composition by Lisa Govan
Cover design by Chip Kidd
Cover photos: PhotoAlto/Alamy (top),
David Leeson/Dallas Morning News/Corbis Sygma (bottom).
First Edition, October 2009

For André Bishop

Prayer for My Enemy

Production History

The world premiere of *Prayer for My Enemy* was co-produced by Intiman Theatre in Seattle, WA (Barlett Sher, Artistic Director; Laura Penn, Managing Director) and Long Wharf Theatre in New Haven, CT (Gordon Edelstein, Artistic Director; Joan Channick, Managing Director). The world premiere production opened at the Intiman Theatre in July 2007 under the direction of Bartlett Sher. The set design was by John McDermott, the lights by Stephen Strawbridge, the costumes by Catherine Zuber and the sound by Stephen LeGrand. The stage manager was Lisa Ann Chernoff and the production manager was Julia L. Collins. The cast was:

BILLY NOONE	Daniel Zaitchik
AUSTIN	John Procaccino
KAREN	Cynthia Lauren Tewes
MARIANNE	Chelsey Rives
TAD VOELKL	James McMenamin
DOLORES ENDLER	Kimberly King
TONY	Conor Gormally

Prayer for My Enemy was originally commissioned by and made its East Coast premiere at the Long Wharf Theatre, where it opened in September 2007 under the direction of Bartlett Sher. The set design was by John McDermott, the lights by Stephen Strawbridge, the costumes by Catherine Zuber and the sound by Stephen LeGrand. The stage manager was Lisa Ann Chernoff. The cast was:

BILLY NOONE	Daniel Zaitchik
AUSTIN	John Procaccino
KAREN	Cynthia Lauren Tewes
MARIANNE	Katie Rose Clarke
TAD VOELKL	James McMenamin
DOLORES ENDLER	Julie Boyd

Prayer for My Enemy made its New York City premiere at Playwrights Horizons (Tim Sanford, Artistic Director; Leslie Marcus, Managing Director) in October 2008 under the direction of Bartlett Sher. The set design was by John McDermott, the lights by Stephen Strawbridge, the costumes by Catherine Zuber, the sound by Scott Lehrer and the music by Nico Muhly. The production stage manager was Lisa Ann Chernoff and the production manager was Christopher Boll. The cast was:

BILLY NOONE	Jonathan Groff
AUSTIN	Skipp Sudduth
KAREN	Michele Pawk
MARIANNE	Cassie Beck
TAD VOELKL	Zachary Booth
DOLORES ENDLER	Victoria Clark

Characters

BILLY NOONE, twenties
AUSTIN, Billy's father, fifties
KAREN, Billy's mother, fifties
MARIANNE, Billy's sister, slightly older than Billy
TAD VOELKL, twenties
DOLORES ENDLER, around forty

Setting

The action takes place in America and Iraq in 2003 and 2004.

Note

Dialogue appearing in italics represents the psychic interior of the character, the running commentary of thoughts and justifications and questions, the emotional tide within, which is not necessarily any more true or reflective of objective reality than the things we actually say out loud; it is simply all the stuff we keep to ourselves, and therefore it includes the lies we tell ourselves. These italicized passages are spoken by the actor, but never heard or responded to by the other characters, except in Scene 12 where indicated.

A slash indicates the point at which the next speaker begins overlapping.

Scene 1

Tad and Billy are both filling their gas tanks.

BILLY: Hey. *(Pause)* Hey.

TAD *(A silent?)*: Huh?

BILLY: How're you doin'? . . . I'm the guy you were tailgating. *(Pause)* Why'd you do that?

TAD: You were going really slow, / look, I—

BILLY: I was driving the speed limit.

TAD: Billy?

BILLY: Tad!? *How long?! Remember? I didn't know you were alive, remember all you did for me, how we talked about Being and Nowhere and the universe and what God might be and how you helped me make it through those years of grade school when I was such a geek getting straight A's and everybody called me a faggot when I wasn't and you said what's wrong with playing with each other until we can get girls and so we did until you started crying that one time and you said you were turning us both gay you couldn't do that to someone so nice, and then your dad got transferred and we said we'd be best friends for life but we weren't, we both kept moving apart and I just assumed somehow you'd gone with guys and I went with women but still there was something so romantic about what happened and I've never told anybody especially with the shit my dad's put me through he went kind of off the deep end or maybe he was always there but anyway wow—*

TAD: You still call me Tad!

BILLY: What do they call you now? Theodore?

TAD: Fuck you! Man, I would've recognized you anywhere, what the fuck's that guy's problem, I thought, better not look him in the eye, that's the only reason it took me so long! *You probably think I just like guys from all that shit back then but I don't I've been married oh it's a long story you're not gonna want to hear, that's why I've moved back.*

BILLY: Where are you living now?

TAD: I've moved back, can you believe it?

BILLY: Your parents? / You—?

TAD: No, I've been married, I got married in high school!

BILLY: *You're straight?*

TAD: Long story.

BILLY: *I feel like I'm gonna cry.*

TAD: Long fuckin' sob story.

(A honk.)

BILLY *(To unseen driver)*: What? We're utilizing the fuckin' services!

TAD: Dude, pull around!

BILLY: Come on, let's both check our oil and drive the fucker crazy.

TAD: No, he's gonna drive around.

BILLY: You look so the fuck the same, what sob story?

TAD: Oh, man.

BILLY: No, come on, I'll buy you a drink.

Scene 2

Tad and Billy are in a bar.

TAD: She was pregnant, you know, I was sure the baby was mine though now, I don't know, we decided to go for it, got married, then she started getting cold feet, you know, adoption, abortion, you sure you want to hear this? So she aborts the baby, I start getting all wigged-out about not maybe going to college, how are we gonna do this, I go on one of those antidepressants, can't practically get it up, she suddenly one day says she has a crush on this other guy, can we try polyamory, you know what that is?

BILLY: Threesomes.

TAD: Bingo, well, she wanted this guy to herself, me to herself, so she goes, starts going back and forth, I get more depressed, more pills, now I can't come even if I could get it up, she leaves me for him, I decide to try a different approach, you know, so I decide to go to one of those retreats, like health yoga in the mountains kind of place where they teach you to let go let, god, I'm drinking like a fish, too, which you're not supposed to do when you're on the other pills, so I give up the pills, but I do it too quick, start hearing voices in my head, back on the pills, go to the retreat, it turns out tantric does not mean learning to medicate, meditate, Jesus, on the breath, it means learn to take the energy you use ejaculating to lighten and I mean would have used, 'cause you stop doing that, you can learn how to not shoot, right?, so that's what I do, I can be really enlightened and energized and concentrated on another person now without, I mean, I can come, I can come like crazy, I can have multiple orgasms, and this drives women wild, but it also makes them kind of nervous about settling down, so I've got this little bevy of beauties, my wife then sues me for mental and emotional cruelty, wins, she wants half the house, my dad bought us the house, she never worked a day in her life, so I sold the house and ran, here I am. What's going on with you?

BILLY: I'm going . . . tomorrow I'm leaving for Iraq.

TAD: *Iraq?*

BILLY: I'm stationed in Baghdad.

TAD: What the fuck are you doing in the military? I thought you'd have a Ph.D. in particle fuckin' physics.

BILLY: Yeah, no, I mean, I decided, you know, I joined the reserves that's all. *I'm not gay!*

TAD: The reserves.

BILLY: Yeah, I don't know. I didn't want to take any more dough from my father, though . . . well, I'm still living at home, but I'm paying rent with the cash from the, anyway, they called us all up, I'm infantry. *He started calling me "Missy" my father, "Missy," "Fagboy," didn't matter how many girls I brought home 'cause I'm not all bluster and I know I'm effeminate, I don't know what the fuck that's got to do with the price of beans, being a fag and being girly they're two different things, it's not like I dress up in women's clothing, I love women but still "Liberace," "Lady William"* —He's out of his mind no I mean really he's crazy, bipolar—

TAD: Your dad?

BILLY: Wouldn't take his meds, the whole family, all we did was try to hold him in place and my older sister married this jackass just to get away from him, my mom spent all her time at the deli it was a fuckin' mess, I joined the reserves thinking he was in Vietnam he'd be, but— What meds?

TAD: Was I on? Lexapro.

BILLY: Yeah, I tried that, same thing: no squirt, but . . .

TAD: You still on it?

BILLY: I'm on some new shit, but I'm not going to be able to get it in Baghdad, fuck, I'm subscribing to all these heavy girly magazines like *Xtreme* just to keep the guys off my back, they started calling me all kinds of shit. *Like "Helen."*

TAD: What kind of shit?

BILLY: Just shit.

TAD: Fuck.

BILLY: *I loved you did you know that?*

TAD: Iraq.

BILLY: I know.

(Pause.)

TAD: What the hell kind a world.

BILLY: They're throwing a going-away thing for me in the back-yard in a little bit, you want to come?

TAD: Oh, I don't to want break in on—

BILLY: No, no, no, you'd be doing me a favor. It's great to see you.

TAD: Yeah! *You were my first love really I don't care what anybody says you were it.* Sure?

BILLY: You'll stop by?

TAD: Yeah, I'm gonna try.

BILLY: Okay. *(Pause)* That's very cool.

(They pummel each other; the tussle becomes an embrace, then they violently shove apart.)

Scene 3

Dolores alone.

DOLORES: Mother didn't want us to postpone the wedding: "It's only a stroke, I'm not an invalid," but that's exactly what she is, long as she needs to be in the wheelchair. Mom says, "I can talk, I can move my arms." As if this were proof of anything. *(Short pause)* Frankly, I'm glad to get out of New York City. Charles, my fiancé, loves all that frenzy, the noise, the endless possibilities. To me, it's one long shriek of rage, that's what I hate most about the city—the fury of so many people's resentment and frustration and, well, they've been put in a space too small for so many, a big filthy loud dangerous ugly unsanitary uncivil and foul-smelling cage. Like rats, they start biting off their own feet, not to mention yours.

9

(Bell.)

Coming! And here I have a clear mission: Keep her occupied, fed, cleaned. It's payback for all the wretched things I put her and Dad through, though to hear them tell it, you'd think I was born a schizophrenic porcupine, or something, instead of a normal—

(Bell.)

Coming! Anyway, Dad's dead, so—

(Bell.)

There must be something wrong. *(Exiting)* Mom? Mom?!

Scene 4

The backyard of Billy's parents' house. Austin is grilling. Tad and Billy are standing with him.

AUSTIN: Their call is different for family members than others outside their clan. Every single elephant in the world, not special ones. All. They perform ceremonies. They can recognize the skeletons of dead relatives . . .

TAD: Uh.

AUSTIN: . . . and they perform a grieving ritual, running their hind feet over the remains, and they sing a grieving song, a heartbreaking noise, nothing else like it on Earth.

BILLY: They have more than one hundred thousand muscles in their trunks alone.

AUSTIN: Highly evolved, their memories are indeed as complex and deep, really, they probably have a larger network of relationships than any other land mammal.

TAD: Huh.

AUSTIN: They do.

(Marianne arrives with a drink for Tad.)

TAD: Thanks.

AUSTIN: What's that?

MARIANNE: *Don't listen to him he's an asshole he'll keep you nailed to this spot for hours and then when you think you've been really nice about it he'll tell you what is wrong with every choice you've ever made.*

AUSTIN: . . . so deep we can't even hear, but from miles away they hear and the sounds have exact meanings, they can tell what one another are thinking.

TAD: That's . . .

MARIANNE: *Boring it's insane a grown man knows all this and—*

(Karen approaches.)

KAREN: How 'bout our soldier boy, hmm?

TAD: You must be very proud. *So cheerful when you're talking about slaughter.*

MARIANNE: *He's made her life impossible refusing to do anything about his / mania.*

TAD: *Off to the morgue her son she raised her only son decapitated probably from some huge piece of flying—and she'd feel so warm and / gooey—*

MARIANNE: *And only when he crashed the / car—*

TAD: *And all their friends and church buddies telling them how wonderful and brave they are!!*

MARIANNE: *Only then does he agree to take his meds and stop drinking and of course lecture everybody about how evolved he is now—*

KAREN *(Looking at Billy)*: He knows how to watch out for himself, I know, so I'm not going to worry.

AUSTIN: I'll give you a documentary to watch. *(Short pause)* On elephants.

TAD: Oh.

BILLY: Oh yeah, we've got them all.

TAD: Great.

KAREN: He's going to be fine. *(To Billy) Why did you enlist? Are you an idiot?! What good are all the things we've taught you and all the things you've learned all the memories you've stored up and all the experiences all the effort and washed cars and finals and after-school work and cleaning your room and French and calculus if you're gonna let it all spill out of your skull with the rest of your brains? / In sand?*

MARIANNE: *And we're supposed to forget that he threw broken appliances at mirrors and stabbed the kiddie pool with a knife when some neighbor kid had peed in it and he was "sick of it goddamn it, what's the point of fighting all the time working I'm sick of / life!"*

BILLY: Okay, enough.

TAD: *God.*

MARIANNE: *Why do you think we never had anyone over?*

TAD: *You always had those little flecks in your eyes, yellow and orange, like a cat. I bet you lick like a cat.*

KAREN: Tad?

TAD: Uh-huh? I'm fine for now, thanks.

(Karen walks away.)

MARIANNE: You look exactly the same.

TAD: I do?

MARIANNE: Doesn't he?

TAD: You look better.

MARIANNE: Oh, I don't think you noticed me back then.

TAD: Are you kidding me?

MARIANNE: No.

TAD: I asked you to the prom.

MARIANNE: No, you didn't.

TAD: I did.

BILLY: He did.

MARIANNE: You did?

AUSTIN: I think he did.

MARIANNE: You all remember that? . . . No, you didn't!

TAD: Okay.

MARIANNE: You did?

TAD: You went with Gerard.

MARIANNE: I married Gerard.

TAD: Oh.

BILLY: You divorced Gerard.

MARIANNE: I divorced Gerard.

TAD: Good. He was kind of an—

MARIANNE: No, we're friends.

TAD: Oh.

MARIANNE: He's okay.

TAD: Yeah, I liked him, okay.

(Pause.)

AUSTIN: They have a kid.

TAD: Oh.

BILLY: *Don't spoil it.*

MARIANNE: *NOOO!*

BILLY: *It's finally working out, can't you see all of what we went through, it's finally straightening out and they're going to be happy and Tad and I and all of us can be friends, we can be a family, and if I for any reason I don't come back she'll have someone to replace everything she's lost already and protect her from you too don't you see that?*

AUSTIN: He's in a home.

MARIANNE: You wanna just speak for me?

AUSTIN: Well, he was wondering, I'm sure.

MARIANNE: Were you?

AUSTIN: Yes he was. *I'm sorry I'm a lunk a lughead, things just come marching out of my mouth, I can't stop them.* —Autistic.

TAD: Yeah?

(Short pause.)

BILLY: He's very beautiful.

MARIANNE: He's very beautiful.

TAD: What's his name?

AUSTIN: Anthony. Tony.   MARIANNE: Tony.

BILLY: He's six.

TAD: What exactly is autism?

MARIANNE: Well, funny you should ask, because no one really knows, they think it might be, well, all kinds of things . . .

AUSTIN: *My fault.*

MARIANNE: . . . but it could be congenital—

(Karen returns with drinks and snacks.)

AUSTIN: That's where I come in, my mental illness.

MARIANNE: He doesn't really respond to love or touch, he's in his own world he can't function in class.

AUSTIN: It runs in my family.

MARIANNE: Go to school.

AUSTIN: I'm bipolar.

TAD: Ah.

KAREN: You're not mentally ill.

AUSTIN: That's why I drank. To take the edge off. *(To Karen, without stopping)* What do you think it is if not a mental illness?

MARIANNE: They think it could also be caused by something as simple as inoculations, / something they use—	KAREN: It's a condition—an allergy.
	AUSTIN: No, alcoholism is an allergy. *(To Tad)* That's what I say if—That's what I say when somebody, whenever anybody offers me a drink.
TAD: I've heard that. *(To Austin)* Uh- / huh.	MARIANNE: Uh- / huh—

AUSTIN: "I'm allergic," I can't. If I drink, I break out in handcuffs.

(Everybody laughs.)

They've all heard that—

MARIANNE: I haven't.

AUSTIN: But— No? I tell people I've used up all the drinks a guy gets allotted for one lifetime, we all get a certain amount . . .

TAD: Uh-huh.

AUSTIN: . . . and I'll tell you, though, this disease doesn't just want to slow me down . . .

TAD: Uh-huh.

AUSTIN: . . . it doesn't want my house, my family, my credit cards, total my car, this disease wants me dead.

TAD: Uh-huh.

AUSTIN: Underground.

TAD: Right.

AUSTIN: It wants me stone-cold done.

TAD: Uh-huh.

AUSTIN: Rotting meat.

TAD: Yeah.   MARIANNE: We get it.

AUSTIN: That's how insidious it is. I'm filled with gratitude. That's what being sober has done for me. I'm blessed with a son, a beautiful kid— And God will protect him, I know. A marvelous daughter, both of them individuals in their own right—

MARIANNE: Thank you.

AUSTIN: —a daughter who puts me to shame with her strength and clarity, don't pooh-pooh me, a loving, endlessly giving wife, they have all given me more than I could possibly ever deserve—

KAREN: Sh.

AUSTIN: I've put them through hell, I have. You can't shut me up. I do, I thank God every day, I hit my knees first and last thing, for this second chance. I didn't deserve it, but . . .

(Short pause.)

MARIANNE: We did.

AUSTIN: I don't ever want to go back.

Scene 5

Dolores alone.

DOLORES: Well, my mom had another stroke. She felt it coming on and kept ringing, I feel awful. Worse still, I called 911 and got that ridiculous recording, "Your call is important to us, please stay on the line." I bundled her up in the car and took her to the emergency room, she's in overnight, at the most two days, it was another tiny one, her vision blacks-out, but she's still awake. Charles wants to put her in a full-time "facility." For Christ's sake, she reads, watches TV; she can cook if I put the cutting board across her wheelchair, she loves to try new things. Last night we were cooking Mexican. Without the chilies. We walk the driveway, she wheels herself . . . And there is no more beautiful time of year than this—the leaves pouring down like feathers from huge unseen flying birds migrating across the sun, so many burnt umbers and oranges and blood, blood reds. Plum colored. The oaks hold on to their leaves the longest, I remember that, even in the shivering bleak cold. That's mother and me, our last holding on. Yes, she can be the world's most gigantic pill, as Charles says, but . . . she's come all this way, through decades, not to mention my dad. I'm the only one now. My sister is way upstate in her—not ashram, silent order: Nuns, Buddhist nuns in Albany, New York, that's like having, I don't know, Kurdish rebels in—Cleveland. But it's just as well she's silent. But mother is quite comfortable. And this is the house I grew up in. Listen:

(Silence.)

That's all you ever hear. A creak when the heat comes up, a corresponding creak when it goes off. I love this house. There is such a sense of . . . fit. You'd think I'd find it oppressive, but . . . I'm less lonely here than I—would be, was, back there, will be again, all too soon. Charles really can't leave the city and I can't see how we can be together if I don't live with him, and I love him— Well, people have many worse problems than this one. But for now I'm getting a little respite, and, oh, for god's sake, we've been sleeping together for seven years. *(Pause)* It isn't that Charles is— The sun doesn't rise and set in his eyes, let's put it that way, he's a human being. He didn't, doesn't quite . . . hang the moon. But he's very responsible and works hard and he's not an a-hole, which in the city, listen, that's more than you might think. To find someone who—especially if you're not nineteen and a micro-neurosurgeon. I started as one of his secretaries at the hospital, he used to be chief of the department. We went out, anyway . . . he's good people.

Scene 6

Billy, Tad and Marianne are together in the backyard, lighting up, smoking a joint.

TAD: What's with the elephants?

BILLY: A lotta people came.

MARIANNE: D'ja think they wouldn't?

BILLY: You know he doesn't talk like that, that's all memorized from documentaries; his father couldn't read. He perseverates.

MARIANNE: Tony . . . does the same thing, but with movies.

TAD: Uh-huh. Perseverate.

MARIANNE: Uh-huh.

BILLY: With Dad it's either elephants or the Yankees.

MARIANNE: Oh, yeah, don't even say that word.

TAD: Okay. "Yankees"?

MARIANNE: He can tell you who played the woman in the tollbooth—

BILLY: Tony.

MARIANNE: Tony, in a chase scene where a car goes crashing through—

BILLY: She doesn't even have to have a close-up.

17

MARIANNE: He knows her name, what other movies she was in . . .

TAD: Mm-hm.

MARIANNE: . . . if she's still alive.

BILLY *(Sees)*: Fireflies.

TAD: I'd like to meet Tony.

BILLY: You should.

MARIANNE: Okay.

BILLY *(Getting up)*: Anybody want?

(Head shakes. Billy moves toward the house. Tad lies back, staring up at the sky.)

MARIANNE: Are you cold?

(Tad shakes his head no.)

TAD: Are you?

(Marianne shakes her head no.)

TAD: Good f[ood]—   MARIANNE: Billy—

MARIANNE: Oh, sorry.

TAD: No.

MARIANNE: Billy joined the reserves, Dad goes: "Great, throw your life away for nothing, oil."

TAD: Uh-huh.

MARIANNE: Billy says something like, "Tell me you don't feel something for kids fighting for you getting killed over in—" and Dad's like, "You don't know anybody over there."

TAD: Uh-huh.

MARIANNE: What were you gonna say?

TAD: Oh, I don't . . . Oh doesn't it seem strange . . . that of all the times it could be, from the beginning of the universe, let's say time isn't infinite, let's say that it's only a couple of hundred trillion years it's all here, then nothing . . . That's still a lot of time. If it could be any little slice of time—

MARIANNE: Yes.

TAD: —any eighty-year slice in all that time—what are the odds—

MARIANNE: Right.

TAD: —that it would be this slice—

MARIANNE: Yes yes.

TAD: —of time that we happen to be alive in . . .

MARIANNE: Uh-huh.

TAD: You've thought this?

MARIANNE: Oh, sure.

TAD: I've tried to explain this to so many people and they never know what I'm getting at.

MARIANNE: No?

TAD: Doesn't it just seem pretty amazing . . .

MARIANNE: Uh-huh.

TAD: . . . that it just happens to be right now—

MARIANNE: Yes.

TAD: —and not during the dinosaurs—

MARIANNE: Absolutely.

TAD: —or a billion years from now when neither of us would be here, it's now, it's right now, in all that vast expanse of time, this is the moment in time it actually is.

MARIANNE: I still can't go to the prom with you.

(Pause.)

TAD: We'll find something to do.

Scene 7

Dolores alone.

DOLORES: Coming back from the hospital, I stopped at the G&K deli, it's been there forever, the same couple running it—

(At the same time, Karen begins to get ready for bed, she washes her face, flosses, etc.)

I've never known their first names, the point is that the wife, Mrs. Noone, always smiles and says hello, recognizing me, which is what's missing in the city. Even if you see the same people over dozens of years, they still act as if you are a threat to their well-being. And is that any place to raise kids? It's fun to drive here, the lakes and the endless woods, serene—

(The sounds of a nature program on public television. Austin kneels by the bed. He prays. But his attention is drawn to the program, the subject of which is naked mole rats.)

Our property even butts up against state park, the Appalachian trail is a thousand feet from the house! But Charles's practice is down there, shrinking heads, unearthing unconscious desires, he makes a pile and he loves what he does, whereas I can do what I do anywhere on Earth. Which is nothing. I mean, I have held down half a dozen jobs over the last fifteen years, but they all seem to be exercises in existential futility: Companies that provide some obscure service, returning profits to unseen people in expensive homes one never gets invited to. I've learned every single word-processing system, computer programming, technological whatever, I can work any phone system with my toes while juggling memos and smiling through the worst nastiness, but why should I have to? Why shouldn't I live like regular people?

KAREN *(To Austin)*: Are you going to stay up?

DOLORES: Charles won't even consider Brooklyn, that's how Manhattan-centric he is. He has his office in the ground-floor space, he has half a brownstone. I've always kept my own eeeny little walkup, and now, with the wedding, we're moving in, oh blah blah blah. Oh, I should get back before visiting hours end, though that's another thing, they don't really care. They don't have all their rules crammed up their asses like—

(Austin and Karen have both gotten into bed. Karen kisses Austin and turns off her light, rolls away from him. The TV light plays on Austin's face.)

One day, New York City has alternate side of the street parking, right? This was back when Charles had the car, so I'm in charge of parking—nice to have a full-time servant, isn't it? I'm waiting for the street cleaner, finally he comes, goes by, and that's another thing: they arrive with this enormous worthless piece of junk that spews dirty water all over everyone and everything, stinking up the atmosphere and leaving the street just as filthy, but now all the shit is wet—that's cleaning the streets in Manhattan—so I re-park the car, get out, and this cop on a mini-toy joke bike, which represents his genitals, I suppose, gives me a ticket! I say, "The street has already been cleaned." He says, "Read the sign." "Oh, come on, that's so they can clean the street, and they have." He says, "I don't make the laws." I wanted to say, "You don't make sense either, and I pay your fucking salary so you can give me tickets for things that aren't hurting anybody, what the fuck is your job anyway, asshole, you think a uniform is a substitute for brains or integrity?" But who needs to get arrested, have you ever seen a holding pen in New York City? They put you in with murderers, no toilets, lock the doors, and go out to lunch on YOUR nickel. I'll take the suburbs. Give me banality before brutality. Any day.

AUSTIN *(Still staring at the TV)*: They lose all their hair and their eyesight; their whole life is lived underground. Look how cute.

Scene 8

Tad speaks with Billy by phone; half of Billy's head is covered with a bandage.

TAD: We miss you, man. Your dad's got me praying and I don't even believe in God!

BILLY: Is anybody on the line?

TAD: What do you mean?

BILLY: Is anybody listening?

TAD: No. Why?

BILLY: I saw him.

TAD: Who?

BILLY: God. I saw God and I saw Satan and I saw past time and this universe, can I tell you, will you just listen?

TAD: What do you mean you saw / God?

BILLY: Okay. Okay, so . . . don't tell anybody, okay?

TAD: Okay.

BILLY: You know I never believed in any of that shit. But okay. Something happened . . . I'll tell you in a letter—

TAD: What?

BILLY: —that's not the important part—the important part is I lost consciousness—

TAD: What happened?

BILLY: I'm okay. I was hit. I got shrapnel in my eye, they got it out.

TAD: Jesus.

BILLY: I'm gonna be a hundred percent.

TAD: Come home, tell 'em you can't see, lie, come on. Nobody thinks you're a coward if you lie, nobody thinks you're not brave or not masculine nobody thinks any of that shit.

BILLY: I could hear and see things, but they were like, I could see through them. I saw that white light everybody talks about and I went into it and past it. I died—and the first thing I realized was, I mean I could see it, this is what God is: There are an infinite number of universes—and time, which we're programmed to perceive—is no more real than anything else— Are you there?

22

TAD: Yeah yeah.

BILLY: I'm telling you something, it's true, this is all real—

TAD: I'm listening.

(Marianne enters.)

MARIANNE: Let me say hi.

BILLY: But things, things that happen here: We're creating them more than we know, okay, listen, please God—

TAD: What?

BILLY: Every fraction of a second the universe splits off into infinite possibilities—ones where I don't drop out, or you and I can grow up to be married to each other, I'm not saying—

TAD: I'm listening, hey.

(Marianne tries to listen in, but Tad moves her away: "Hang on.")

BILLY: It's all choice, okay, and I was even starting to decompose, stuffing my hands into the soil, and I tried to stand and I realized that there is nothing substantial about the body, I threw myself on a bush with strong branches and I passed through it, first the branches stung like hell and then I just let go, I let my body go—

TAD: Uh-huh.

BILLY: Right through it. You know how we have consciousness? We're always moving a little bit forward and a little bit back, we conceive of everything in terms of then and now, and that's an illusion! A seizure is just rapid moving between then and now, then and now—

TAD: Did you have one?

BILLY: I died, man.

MARIANNE *(Mouthed or sotto voce)*: Have what?

BILLY: And I was onto another world when I started to ache for the people I love, Mom and Marianne and you and my buddies . . . *Dad* . . . I chanted their names and moved back through all the stages, back into this world, you know, like someone who chooses to be reborn so they can help others,

I wanted to find out how all your stories come out, I mean, I wanted to help and love you all.

TAD: Come home, okay?

BILLY: I will.

TAD: I gotta see your fuckin' face.

BILLY: I will.

TAD: You gotta go back to school, you gotta write this shit down, you gotta—

BILLY: I will. / But—

MARIANNE: Let me . . .

TAD: Hold on.

MARIANNE *(Takes the phone)*: Hey.

BILLY: Hey.

MARIANNE: Did he tell you?

BILLY: What?

MARIANNE: You sitting down?

BILLY: What?

MARIANNE: We're, you're gonna be an uncle.

BILLY: Hey!

MARIANNE: Yeah.

BILLY: How about that?!?

MARIANNE: Are we nuts?

BILLY: Oh!—

(Billy cries.)

MARIANNE: What a zoo, huh? I'm gonna try and give you a normal one this time. Nephew.

TAD: Don't say that.

BILLY: It's a boy?

MARIANNE: I'm just—yeah. Hey. So . . . thanks for bringing your friend over! Are you . . . ?

BILLY: I'm so good.

MARIANNE: We love you, are you okay?

BILLY: That is— Oh, congratulations.

MARIANNE: Yeah.

BILLY: I'm sorry.

MARIANNE: So. Here, I'll give him back.

TAD: No.

MARIANNE: Oh, well—

BILLY: It's okay.

MARIANNE: Mom and Dad both send their love.

BILLY: Are they there?

MARIANNE: No. I mean . . .

BILLY: Okay, well—give 'em my love.

MARIANNE: You, too.

BILLY: And I'll call—

MARIANNE: Theo'll tell me what's going on.

BILLY: Okay.

MARIANNE: Okay? / So.

BILLY: Okay.

MARIANNE: You're sure you're okay?

BILLY: I love you!

MARIANNE: You're sure you're—? Love you, too!

(Billy hangs up.)

Aww.

TAD: Don't say that.

MARIANNE: Oh, I don't know, I'm just . . . He cried. Like a baby.

TAD: Well sure. Life. That's gotta be . . .

MARIANNE: I know.

TAD: Don't say that about Tony.

MARIANNE: I know.

TAD: I love him just as much as—

MARIANNE: I know. I don't know. What is it with men? You get so emotional. *(Pause)* Okay.

Scene 9

Dolores alone.

DOLORES: "My mother is dying," I said, "please come up." And he says, "Honey, she's in a coma, she doesn't even know

25

you're there, hop on the train!" Hop on the train? You, hop on this, you . . . *(Pause)* I keep getting in the car, driving over, driving back, there's nothing to do, I don't want to leave her alone, but— And everyone is so nice, the head nurse, all the staff, even the cleaning people smile and say, "Excuse me." But it is really . . . so beautiful right here right now, why didn't I know that growing up? I'm so attuned to everything, the beauty, Mom holding on to her life, bit by bit, all of it, the past and the present, it's all so . . . unbelievably rich. *(Pause)* "Hop on the train." I'd like to hop on your fucking head and suffocate you with my thighs and whatever else you don't pay enough attention to, you're so tired and . . . Ugh. Listen to me.

(Phone.)

Oh god, here it comes. *(Into phone)* Hello? . . . Oh! Thank you. Thank you very much. *(Hangs up)* She woke up!

Scene 10

Austin, Tad and Billy in front of the TV: the sixth game of the American League Championship between the Red Sox and the Yankees; bottom of the eighth. Karen and Marianne, visibly pregnant, are in the kitchen. The action moves back and forth between these two rooms and a corner of the dining room where there is a liquor cart.

BILLY: Shake my hand.
AUSTIN: Come on.
BILLY: See? Already you insulted me. You pulled away first. They look you in the eye. They want to feel your spirit. It's the cradle of civilization.
TAD: The Garden of Eden, I read that: right in Iraq.

(The umpire calls Rodriguez out, and Jeter is forced to return to first base.)

AUSTIN: He didn't mean to knock it out—

TAD: Yes, he did.

AUSTIN: He was just running.

TAD: Look at it. He knocks it, there. They're too freaked-out and getting desperate.

AUSTIN: Oh, come on!

BILLY: Game, Dad, it's not real. Nobody's gonna die.

(Karen comes in with snacks.)

AUSTIN: Oh, he goes abroad, now he's the He-Man.

KAREN: Stop that, you know you're proud of him; he's risking his life.

AUSTIN: I didn't say he didn't risk his life. I said killing people isn't the same as courage.

(Austin exits for the bathroom, off.)

KAREN: It's the Yankees.

BILLY: Don't they know they can't lose? Our family's equilibrium depends on them.

KAREN: If only it were a joke.

BILLY: He's fine.

KAREN: He's very worried about you.

TAD: Can we help?

KAREN: Can the Yankees really lose?

BILLY: They are losing.

MARIANNE *(Entering)*: I hope they lose. I hope they're ground to dust.

KAREN: Shhh.

MARIANNE: I hope the Yankees go out of business. I hope we never watch or have to listen to another game as long as we live. I hope he has to hang his head in shame—

KAREN: Stop it.

MARIANNE: —and stop terrorizing us with his ignorance.

AUSTIN *(From off)*: I'm sorry, I'm upset! I apologize!

BILLY: It's okay.

MARIANNE: Why is it okay? It's not okay.

KAREN: Stop it.

MARIANNE: I hate him.

KAREN: Stop it, everyone. We're together. Billy's home. We're alive, can't we be grateful.

MARIANNE: Tell him. He pulls me aside to tell me Tad's an alcoholic. We're married now, I'm pregnant.

KAREN: He's just trying to protect everybody.

(Flush. Austin returns.)

AUSTIN: I'm sorry, I was wrong; it was wrong. Do you accept that?

MARIANNE: Sure.

(Marianne exits. Austin turns the sound up on the game.)

AUSTIN: Look how complicated life is! I mean, what a— Televisions! Computers! Modern warfare. Hey, I didn't mean you aren't . . .

BILLY: I know.

AUSTIN: You know I love you.

BILLY: I know.

TAD: But if life is so complicated and amazing that there has to be a God . . . then who made God? How come you can't accept the idea that life and the universe have always been here, that all this marvelous complexity couldn't be without a God, but something even more marvelous and complex and all-encompassing than this, God, doesn't have to have some explanation.

AUSTIN: Faith defies logic.

TAD: It sure does.

(Pause.)

AUSTIN: Look at this sorry-assed . . .

BILLY: I haven't. I haven't killed anyone.

(Pause.)

TAD: I'm glad.
BILLY: I haven't killed anyone.
AUSTIN: What?
TAD: He hasn't killed anyone.

(Pause.)

BILLY: You should know that.
AUSTIN: It's good news.

(Pause. Billy gets up and moves into the kitchen.)

(Regarding the game) Look at this shit.
TAD: How we must puzzle the angels, huh?
AUSTIN: The Angels?
TAD: Above.
AUSTIN: Oh.
TAD: Marianne always says that. How we must puzzle the angels.
AUSTIN: Yeah.

(Billy, Karen and Marianne in the kitchen. Billy uses his laptop.)

BILLY: He had this camera with this incredible lens, you know, and tripod; he could take pictures in almost total darkness, and you can't make any light where we were, they see you light a cigarette and blam you're in their sites, you're done.
KAREN: Oh my god.
BILLY: So he wants to do this portrait of me in the moonlight, right, and he sets it all up, tells me how to cock my head, where to look and he presses the button, he's forgotten to turn off the flash.
MARIANNE: Oh no.
BILLY: It took his head off.
KAREN: What?

BILLY: The missile.

MARIANNE: In front of you?

BILLY: That's, a piece of that, what got my eye.

KAREN: Oh, don't say anymore.

MARIANNE: Why didn't you write us?

BILLY: I have the picture. It came out. I'm looking so serene. One like fraction infinitesimal fraction of a second before this guy's head, I mean—

KAREN: Please.

BILLY: And we go off into different universes in that tiny blink—

MARIANNE: You're lucky it hit your eye.

BILLY: Lucky? Oh, you mean instead of my heart.

MARIANNE: No. Well, yes, but no, I mean, if you'd just stayed standing there, watching, you had your own things to worry about.

KAREN: What's this?

BILLY: The picture.

KAREN: Oh, I don't want to see it.

MARIANNE: He's fine in it.

KAREN: I know.

(Karen moves out of the room.)

MARIANNE: She doesn't understand how that makes you feel, not wanting to see it. She doesn't think you're bringing her death—

BILLY: Yes, she does.

MARIANNE: No, you feel that—you've brought it home. It's written all over you, that you feel that.

BILLY: That isn't the way it's happening.

MARIANNE: Is it true we blew up the hospital in Fallujah so there wouldn't be a way to know how many casualties there were?

BILLY: Where did you hear that? No.

MARIANNE: Somebody came into the deli.

BILLY: You're working?

MARIANNE: Of course.

BILLY: Who said that?

MARIANNE: Some lady I didn't know, she saw I was watching the news, she said it.

BILLY: It's bad. But it's not bad like that.

MARIANNE: How is it bad?

KAREN *(Reentering)*: Let him put it behind.

BILLY: Let you put it behind.

KAREN: No. I didn't mean that.

BILLY: It's bad because somebody forgets to tell the Iraqis we have a curfew and somebody steps out to get a coffee and one of ours blows him away. It's bad because when we run out of cigarettes we break into their houses and pretend it's a raid and we're looking for guns but we're just stealing their cigarettes. It's bad because the insurgents are the people who live there. Probably. It's bad because it was bad before we got there and now it's bad in a new way.

(Pause.)

KAREN: I see. Well, you never have to see any of it ever again.

BILLY: *I'm going back.*

MARIANNE: Something's wrong. Yes, it is. What?

KAREN: What?

BILLY: Nothing.

KAREN: Let's go watch your father's game. And be ready to shore him up.

MARIANNE: I'll be right in.

BILLY: Me, too.

(Karen moves to the TV room.)

MARIANNE: Did you volunteer to go back?

BILLY: We got a new commanding officer once we moved south and he wants combat on his record, so I'm going back.

MARIANNE: Why can't they send new people?

BILLY: Because I'm in his battalion, I have more time.

MARIANNE: But with what happened to your eye?

BILLY: Shhhh.

MARIANNE: You almost lost it.

BILLY: It would have been better if I did.

MARIANNE: No.

BILLY: Shh. Let me see the ultrasound.

MARIANNE: It's not fair.

BILLY: They can hear. *(Looks at the ultrasound pictures)* Look at that!

MARIANNE: His little balls?

BILLY: Why are you working?

MARIANNE: What else am I gonna do?

BILLY: Is Dad not working?

(Head shake.)

Why?

MARIANNE: Why do you think?

BILLY: Has he had a . . . ?

MARIANNE: No, but she's worried, we're all worried.

BILLY: He's not drinking?

MARIANNE: He's stopped going to meetings.

BILLY: It's all been so good. For so long.

MARIANNE: Things have a habit of not staying the same, have you noticed?

(Tad, Austin and Karen are in front of the TV.)

TAD: You had a lot of years of winning. And they've waited how many years? Eighty?

KAREN: Six.   AUSTIN: Let 'em wait.

TAD: A lot of people think the Yankees bought their way to the top and that's no way to keep winning. Maybe it's karma. I mean, that's a long curse.

AUSTIN: *You're on something besides alcohol, aren't you? I see it in your eyes. You're flushed, you're sailing on something. You can't face becoming a father. You can't stop thinking she's gonna have another autistic one, your whole life is gonna be tethered to failure and toilets flushing. And you're right. We'll never have more than the little we eke out of the deli, bought our way to the top. You should be so lucky. It costs you and costs you. I saw babies raped in Vietnam, I saw children on fire, you try it on. You couldn't do what Billy's doing. You put your mitts all over my daughter and come in here and talk about the Yankees!? Suck my fuckin' dick.*

KAREN: They'll pull through, you watch. They won't lose.

(They watch the game. It is the top of the ninth inning. Billy returns from the kitchen, sits. Everyone watches the game. Marianne, alone in the kitchen, eats pie directly from the pie tin.)

MARIANNE: *He wouldn't have enlisted if you'd ever made him feel like a man. Mother wouldn't have had to represent you if you'd spoken your own damn piece, if you'd taken any responsibility for your own feelings and said how proud you were; she had to do it and she hates war. You're the only one who likes waving your big fat veteran ass around so everybody can see it, why don't you go kill some animals or something and work it out?! Is that true? Is any of that true?*

(Marianne returns to the TV room, still eating.)

Would someone tell me the truth? Someone tell me what's true. I can't sort it, I can't sort anything out.

TAD: Are you all right?

MARIANNE: I'm great. Our family's here. Everything's great.

AUSTIN: Are you being sarcastic?

MARIANNE: *What is wrong with you?! Everyone hates you.*

TAD *(To Billy)*: Hey, let me show you something.

AUSTIN: You aren't going to watch?

TAD: You keep the plane up.

(Tad and Billy go into the dining room. Tad offers Billy a pill.)

Want one?

BILLY: What is it?

TAD: Ecstasy.

BILLY: Did you take one?

TAD: About half an hour ago.

BILLY: Sure, why not.

TAD: It's good stuff.

BILLY: Is everything okay?

TAD: When can we talk?

BILLY: Why?

TAD: I want to know how you are. All that shit about God, seeing God.

BILLY: Oh, I know. Did I freak you out?

TAD: Were you on drugs?

(Head shake.)

I kept writing you.

BILLY: I was afraid they'd see my email.

TAD: Marianne? She doesn't read my email.

BILLY: I didn't know. You were never by yourself when I called.

TAD: Oh, come on!

(They embrace.)

I love you.

BILLY: I love you, too.

TAD: We're family now.

BILLY: We're family.

TAD: This is good stuff.

BILLY: Okay. Thanks.

TAD: No more God shit.

BILLY: Okay.

TAD: Come on.

(They return to the TV room.)

KAREN: Well. We'd better start praying for the Sox.

TAD: You've come over to my side?

KAREN: No. So we don't resent them. It's an AA thing. Somebody hurts you, you pray for them.

TAD: Really?

AUSTIN: Why, is that so strange?

TAD: It's—no, it's—no.

AUSTIN: Makes good sense. Rather than sitting there, stewing, or building up a case against, maybe you should think about it.

TAD: Maybe I should.

AUSTIN: Pray for me.

TAD: I don't resent you. Austin. I love you.

KAREN: He loves you, too, we all do.

MARIANNE: *Love love love.*

BILLY: What's the score?

AUSTIN: The same.

KAREN: Four-two.

TAD: What would I resent you for?

MARIANNE: Calling you a drunk?

KAREN: I'm going to bed if everyone doesn't stop. This is a celebration. Our son is home.

MARIANNE: *Not for long.*

KAREN: Our family is all together, and a new one on the way!

(Cabrera steals second.)

AUSTIN: Get him! Get him! Get him! Wake up! It's finished.

KAREN: We have a whole half inning still. Please everybody.

BILLY *(To Karen)*: You work so hard holding it all together.

KAREN: No, I don't.

BILLY: You're heroic.

KAREN: Oh, stop it! You've just come back from . . .

BILLY: When the shit is flying, it's not like you're making a choice. There's no choosing. You know this, Dad—

AUSTIN: Shh.

BILLY: The military is about no thinking. What is it Dad says? Stay out of your head, it's a bad neighborhood.

AUSTIN: My family's more AA than I am.

BILLY: *Whoa. I feel it. Could I feel it already? I'm rolling.*

MARIANNE: What are you two smiling about?

AUSTIN: They're having a love affair.

MARIANNE: 'Least someone is.

(Marianne gets up and exits.)

KAREN: Okay, good night.   AUSTIN: Stay.

(Tad follows Marianne into the dining room.)

TAD: What are you doing?

MARIANNE: Counting to a million.

TAD: Is he driving you crazy?

MARIANNE: Can I tell you something? Billy's going back.

TAD: What?

MARIANNE: They're making him go back.

TAD: He has like one month left.

MARIANNE: They can extend it somehow, I don't know.

TAD: No. No no no no.

MARIANNE: I know. Shhh.

TAD: Oh god.

MARIANNE: I know.

TAD: He's going to be all right.

MARIANNE: I have never wanted a drink more . . .

TAD: You're almost there. You're almost at the finish line.

MARIANNE: *You're?*

TAD: Okay?

MARIANNE: *Not, "We're"?*

TAD: Okay?

MARIANNE: Okay.

(He embraces her.)

"You're almost there"?

TAD: We're going to be okay.

MARIANNE: Yes, we are. Of course we are.

(They rejoin the others in front of the TV. Commercials play before the bottom of the ninth inning begins.)

AUSTIN: We held the line.

TAD: Oh, thank god. If you hadn't held the line, Austin . . .

KAREN: Still four-two.

MARIANNE: It's exciting. What would be the point if it weren't neck and neck? Something to keep us excited.

KAREN: Not too excited.

AUSTIN: Yes, Mother.

MARIANNE: *What a great setup you've got for yourself. You get your "serenity" and the rest of us have to walk on pins and needles to the last of our days so you don't slip up, and just in case we forget and do something the way we want, have our own lives, Tad drinks, so what, you start to manifest your little symptoms, your old you, so we all fall into line.*

TAD: I saw Tony.

MARIANNE: When?

TAD: Today. On my way home from work.

MARIANNE: Why didn't you tell me?

TAD: I'm telling you now.

BILLY: *Be careful, this drug, I remember: It makes you think everything is safe, no feeling or thought is too dangerous to say, but that's the drug.*

TAD: We just sat.

MARIANNE: I wish I'd known.

TAD: Well, let's go now.

MARIANNE: We can't go now, I'm just saying—*I miss when a kiss didn't have so many consequences.*

BILLY: *Days of pure waiting, nothing but waiting, you can't move, you can't speak—*

AUSTIN: *Drink. One drink.*

KAREN: *There isn't a player on that field I wouldn't want to see naked.*

(Mueller pops to shortstop.)

AUSTIN: Fuck me! Yes! Yes!

TAD: Last chance.

AUSTIN: Who wants a drink?

KAREN: No.

AUSTIN: I'm asking others.

MARIANNE: We're fine. We're all fine.

AUSTIN: I'm having a glass of water.

(He goes into the kitchen. Karen waits a beat, then follows. Austin drinks from a bottle of spring water.)

KAREN: Me, too, please.

AUSTIN: Hell, have a real drink.

(He pours her something strong.)

There you go.

KAREN: Thank you. Cheers.

AUSTIN: I'll be right in. Stop policing me. I've been sober six years.

KAREN: Okay, I just wanted to . . .

AUSTIN: Spy.

KAREN: Be with you.

AUSTIN: *Liar.*

(Karen returns to the TV room. Austin sniffs from the bottle of whatever he poured for Karen, then closes it up without having any. Marianne brings in Tad to talk with Austin.)

TAD: Austin?

AUSTIN: Yeah.

TAD: I don't want you worried about me. I'll go to a meeting with you if you're worried.

AUSTIN: You don't quit drinking for somebody else.

MARIANNE: Then why do you browbeat people if that isn't what you want?

AUSTIN: It isn't I don't want it, it's he's gotta want it.

MARIANNE: He just offered to go with you.

AUSTIN: That's very good. That's nice.

(Tad and Marianne follow Austin back into the TV room.)

BILLY: *They're coming into your house, somebody said you're hiding someone and there's shouting, guns go off, you don't know who's been shot in the next room, you reach for something to defend yourself, but somebody comes in before you can get it and sees you and you're splatter paint, no more, it's quick, the way a pet makes a dash for the open door, they're out, they're gone in a flash.*

AUSTIN: If you'd like to come with me, I'd be happy to take you. The guys, around here anyway, they tend not to be as smart as you or Marianne, Billy, it's— Look, I'm just saying.

TAD: Can I see some literature?

AUSTIN: Sure. Anytime.

TAD: I'd like that.

(Pause.)

MARIANNE *(Regarding the game)*: Last chance.

(Austin looks at her.)

I say it to torment you.

(They all watch.)

Last chance, last chance.

KAREN: It'll be nice for them to go to the series for once. We should be happy for them.

AUSTIN: I don't know any of you people.

TAD: Billy's going back. He's afraid to tell you, his tour has been extended, a lot of guys just like him, they have to go back for one more stint, this'll be the last. And he's gonna be okay. He's afraid to tell you.

39

BILLY: I thought I'd wait until . . .

AUSTIN: We'd lost?

BILLY: I thought I'd spend a little more time with you—

AUSTIN: Why wait?

MARIANNE: You can lie, can't you? Say you can't see! Say you're gay.

BILLY: And leave my buddies to die for the rest of us?

AUSTIN: See? He wants to go.

BILLY: It's not that simple.

AUSTIN: Hell, it's not!

(Austin walks toward the liquor, takes a bottle of vodka into the kitchen and pours a tall glass. He downs it during:)

KAREN *(About Billy)*: How can they do that?

MARIANNE: Daddy's having a drink, I know it.

KAREN: Austin?

AUSTIN: Two seconds!

BILLY: Dad?

AUSTIN: Be right in! I'm fine!

KAREN: You knew?

MARIANNE: I just found out.

(Pause.)

BILLY: I'm sorry.

KAREN: It's not your fault. Bad timing.

TAD: How could he risk his life some more when the Yankees are losing? It's unfortunate.

MARIANNE: Tad.

TAD: Marianne.

(Austin returns with his glass refilled.)

AUSTIN: That's a bad break, Son, I'm sorry.

(Austin finishes his drink. He reaches for a book, opens it and shows it to Tad.)

You see that? All those underlined words? I look up how to pronounce them so I won't be like the rest of the boneheads at my meetings. I didn't have what he has. I was drafted and when I got back from Vietnam I had to work at the deli or we'd lose it. I have to look things up that he knows in his sleep.

TAD: I thought it was her father's deli.

AUSTIN: Yeah, and? I still had to work if they were gonna keep it. But he didn't have to do that, see? He didn't have to fight. He wanted to.

BILLY: *And no one is proud of me.*

AUSTIN: Right?

(Pause. Sierra walks; Matsui to second.)

KAREN: There. There you go! There's still hope!

(They watch the game in silence. Austin rises.)

Where are you going?

AUSTIN: I'm gonna catch a meeting.

KAREN: Now?

AUSTIN: We've lost.

KAREN: We've got a man on third.

AUSTIN: We're gonna lose.

(Austin leaves the house. Tad, Marianne, Karen and Billy sit, unmoving. Karen sniffs Austin's drink.)

Scene 11

Dolores in great distress, phone to ear.

DOLORES: Yes, I'm here. Yes. Mitsubishi. Station wagon, I don't know what year, it's my mother's and she's in the hospital, I went to visit her last night, and I've just woken up to realize it's gone, I must have left the keys in the car, because I can't find them. Yes. That's right. Well, I'm not going anywhere until I get the car back, I suppose. All right.

(She hangs up, pours herself a strong drink.)

Please oh please, Jesus Christ, our lord . . . I was looking forward to driving back from the hospital, she was sitting up and drinking her tea, getting ready to go back to sleep, the sun wasn't up, and I love this time of day, particularly with the lakes all smooth and the birds calling to each other, and the first thing that happens, the very first stoplight, this . . . moron behind me is in such a hurry to turn right, on red, that he pulls right up my ass and starts flicking his lights. I don't know what got me, but I slammed on my breaks, without even thinking, and he practically hits me, starts leaning on his horn, and . . . I don't know, I had had it, really, one thing about the country is the peace, the lack of honking, one doesn't need to get killed just going outside, so when he tries to pass me—this is a windy road—I start pulling left, feigning right, and now he's really really mad—I can't see his face or what make of car, it's one of those awful truck-like things with their lights up high so when you're driving at night you're completely blinded while they're looking down on the rest of the world from their armored tanks, smashing you and your car to bits and they walk away unscathed. Anyway, whenever we reach a curve, and there are other cars coming by, one or two, I go incredibly slowly, like as slowly as I can without actually stopping, I'm sure steam is coming out of his ears and he's honking and weaving, and we do this for what seems like forever.

(She sips. Silence.)

My god almighty Jesus. Finally, I've had my fun and I'm starting to think, He's probably got a gun, everybody does up here except me. Dad did, Mom got rid of it, I pull over

on the straightaway near the boat basin and he roars around
in front of me and slams on his brakes. Do I honk? Do I flick
my brights in his mirror, well, I may have, but then I wait
for him to pull ahead and as quickly as I possibly can I whip
around and head back toward the hospital, even though it
means I'm going to have to go like eighteen miles out of my
way, because there is no road going east-west between—
whatever—he turns around, and now I'm spooked, so . . .
senselessly I pull off on this mining road where we all used
to go walking with Dad, and I know that I can get to the
Appalachian trail from there, because Beth and I used to
walk up over the mountain, and over this rushing stream
there's a waterfall, and after about three hours you come to
the back of our property, so I've been. This is years ago. And
I pull off in the bushes where I know I can hide, and he roars
past me, thank god, but then I hear his brakes squeal, and
I'm stuck in mud, I can't back up. It's a nightmare, I keep
thinking I'm going to wake up, I run out of the car, leave it
unlocked, start up this rise where I know there's the old
ruins of a camp, an outdoor fireplace, I think it must have
been a hunter's cabin at one time, the foundation is still
there, and a thousand used condoms. I charge up to the top
and I hear this lunatic chasing after me, I hear his steps in
the leaves, and so . . . I don't know how I thought of this,
but I knew he was going to kill me if I didn't do something.
I started dropping little pebbles off the top of the . . . thing,
the . . . precipice, down into the underbrush, I'm behind the
fireplace, and damn it if he doesn't head in there, thinking
it's me, and then . . . I realized . . . that wasn't going to work
for very long, so when he was there I . . . picked up one enormous stone, the biggest I could carry, and dropped it over
the edge. It missed him, and I saw him look up—he was, his
face was wide open like a pan— Who is that? Do I know
him?!?!—I just pushed what remained of the fireplace over,
and it fell, like a prop wall in a Buster Keaton movie. He'd
started to run out from under me, but not in time, the stones
hit the ground and, of course, his head, and . . . what a

sound . . . he's moaning. I realize there were cars that saw us, I could easily be identified, so I threw the keys into the woods, went back to the car, wiped the steering wheel down, though why I did that . . . My prints would be on the steering wheel of my own car . . . and I walked back on the Appalachian trail. No one. Just the deer. And I was more frightened than they were. And then I remembered: He's the man from the G&K deli. His son is in Iraq. Oh. I had enough time to think what to do . . . I buried my clothes, my shoes and muddy pants, at the bottom of Mother's mulch pile and I called 911. —Yes indeedie: "Your call is important to us," and I report a stolen car, gone for some part of the night, I didn't hear it turn over, I was sleeping, I have a white-noise machine, I have a sick mother, I really need my car, please, anything you can do. Give them the license plate, they say they'll call, but stolen cars are often never found, they go out of state, they repaint them.

(Pause.)

So I guess I can wait. I'm going to take one of Mother's librium. That way, if they come over, I can act the way innocent people do. Calm and . . . ignorant.

Scene 12

A hospital room. Austin, his face in bandages, his skin the same color of the bandages, attached to an IV, monitors, etc. Billy in uniform and Karen by the bed. The beep of the heart monitor. Karen tries to comfort Billy who moves away from her. Eventually, she leaves. Billy massages and extends Austin's fingers, working the atrophied muscles of the hands.
Dolores appears at the door with a potted plant.

DOLORES: Oh.

BILLY: Hi.

DOLORES: I'm Dolores Endler whose car . . . was—

BILLY: Of course, come in.

DOLORES: Is your mother . . . ?

BILLY: She just went home, have a seat. Please.

DOLORES: This is for . . .

BILLY *(Taking the plant)*: Thank you. That's very kind of you. We were sorry to hear about your mother. The nurses / told us.

DOLORES: Yes, well—I would have been by sooner.

BILLY: Oh, you never had to . . .

DOLORES: Of course I did. You never expect these sorts of thing to happen in the country.

(Pause. Beeps.)

What do they think, do they say, are his chances of coming out of the coma? . . .

BILLY: Less and less with time.

DOLORES: God.

(Pause.)

BILLY: It's so nice of you to be concerned.

DOLORES: Oh, no. You know what I think? I think he saw someone stealing my car, the police said he was out driving, and he chased them, and the person panicked and he followed them into the woods and . . . That's what I think. He's died, I mean, oh, I'm so sorry—

BILLY: That's all right.

DOLORES: This happened because he's a hero. That's what I believe. There are so few. True heroes. Except, well . . . people like you.

The cops said you'd be surprised how often things like this happen and someone gets away with it.

BILLY: Yeah. My sister says that's all we do, men. Is get away with it. And women run around wiping up the blood.

DOLORES: Well, not your dad. Not to me.

(Pause.)

Are you two close?

BILLY: I was supposed to fix him.

DOLORES: They say they can hear you even if they can't speak.

BILLY: He's not gonna start hearing me now.

DOLORES: Maybe he will. Maybe he can now with . . .

BILLY: How am I gonna fix him if I can't go along? It's my job. My mission. He won't know what to do.

(Dolores and Billy are both seated, looking away from the hospital bed. Austin opens his eyes and painfully brings himself to a sitting position. The heart monitor beeping has stopped. Dolores does not react to Austin or see him. However, Billy does, turning to listen to Austin at times, receiving his entire speech as if hearing his father from within the coma.)

AUSTIN: *Listen and shut up. There are things people get too embarrassed to say and those are the only things the measure of a man and I know because I couldn't I had urges and couldn't overcome but you have discipline you have muscles in your head I don't these are the things: Charity. Civility. Sacrifice. Contemplation. Don't smirk; all wisdom is plagiarism, only stupidity is original. There is no reason we should allow our embarrassment to kill us that's what I did I was embarrassed and so I threw away one whole and perfect existence that's what my father did and I watched and followed and you listen to me now; there is no reason you can't know what human beings have known for all of time there is no reason you can't act: precious things lead us astray. Do not succumb. Speak respectfully to people especially your elders, you think we've got eternity to get this right, we get one trip, in and out, a blank sheet a perfect white screen and we rub our shitty mess around on it and think that's a life, hell is truth seen too late, it is better to give than to receive, for me not somebody else; what in the world did we think would happen? Racing and hurrying madden the mind, never, never hit a woman a child keep your eyes open when kissing and listen attentively to your opposition listen to everything the air listen to gravity the pull.*

(Austin turns and sees Dolores for the first time, just at the moment she turns to look at him. They lock gazes. He starts to move toward her, then stops.)

Charity. Civility.

(Austin climbs back into bed, begins to lie down again.)

And if you're traveling in a group of three and someone makes a suggestion for what to do or where to go next always say yes. They'll love you for it. When in doubt stop. Do nothing. It's always better. Say yes. Do nothing . . . stop . . .

(Everything restores; the beep of the heart monitor resumes. Neither Billy nor Dolores acknowledges what has happened.)

DOLORES: Are you back for good?

(Billy shakes his head.)

Oh. It must be difficult hating people you don't even know.
BILLY: Not really.
DOLORES: You mustn't be shocked. If you're relieved . . . some part of you wants him . . . For instance—well, I'm talking about myself—my "fiancé" Charles couldn't inconvenience himself to come to my mother's memorial. "Important conference." And that made me realize: Hooray! Good riddance. But. What do we do when our mortal enemy just ups and disappears. What would you do if the Iraqis just walked away?
BILLY: That's a funny way to think of it.
DOLORES: I've just come from the lawyer. And who would have thought my mother had so much money!
BILLY: Yeah?

DOLORES: And leave it to me! In the will she wrote my sister won't need an income given her vows of poverty and silence. She's a Buddhist nun, but I think it's hilarious she put that in, as if Mom was saying, "Well, if you'd spoken up, honey, I'd have stuck you in!" I should be shipped off in a cage for cannibals to eat.

BILLY: You're just in mourning.

DOLORES: You must see a lot. I mean, be able to. Don't you? . . . I think if we look at people, simply look directly at them, we see who they are. You see who I am. I see you seeing me . . . We see.

(Billy and Dolores stare at one another. And stare.)

BILLY: We're not here to judge each other.

DOLORES: . . . You have a girlfriend?

BILLY: I'm on a generic antidepressant they're giving me over there, I can't really have sex. To anyone's satisfaction.

(The monitor stops beeping, flatlines.)

DOLORES: What's that?

(Billy moves from his chair.)

Is that bad?

(Billy sticks his head out into the hall.)

BILLY: Nurse? Somebody?

Scene 13

Dolores alone.

DOLORES: Why did I do that? I almost confessed to that child! What the hell would that have accomplished? Even if he suspects, he can't prove it. And what was his father doing in the woods at that hour of the night anyway? I have no motive! What, I was angry! And afraid! I didn't mean to hurt him! Oh, of course I did. I meant to shut him up for good, I meant to punish him for being there at all! So that's who I am. That's who I am. Now what? What would you do? Come clean? Pay the price, whatever it is? Because, you see, I can't assume I'll be forgiven. No no no. I could spend hundreds of thousands of dollars on lawyers to prove it was self-defense and still spend years of my life behind bars! Not to mention putting those poor people through the hell of names plastered everywhere, trials, and on top of everything they've already been through, would any of it bring him back? No! It would feel better for me to confess, so I could do the right thing! Hooray! And throw my life away. First thing . . . first thing: Forgive myself. Do they even teach you how to do that? Where is all this forgiveness everyone is always talking about? Have you seen it? Because I haven't. Honestly, no wonder everybody's taking something, I am. It lifts all the—everything . . . "Leave a room cleaner than you found it," that's what my dad always said. I keep . . . Leave a room cleaner than you found it, if all else fails . . . Leave a room cleaner than you found it.

Scene 14

Before the memorial. Karen and Marianne are in the dining area, pouring drinks. Tad and Billy stand apart; Tad has a sleeping newborn in a sling. Austin's casket stands at the back of the room.

MARIANNE: How's your sinus?
KAREN: I took two more pills.
MARIANNE: Watch, with the alcohol. You look beautiful.
KAREN: Thank you. So do you.

(Dolores enters with food.)

DOLORES: Hey.
KAREN: Dolores!

(They hug.)

You've been a godsend.
DOLORES: Ohhhhh. Well, put me to work.
KAREN *(Heading toward the kitchen)*: I don't know, I think we're almost set . . .

(Marianne and Karen exit; Dolores sees Billy staring at her.)

DOLORES: Hi, handsome.

(Billy turns his back to her and walks away. Dolores uneasily slips off into the kitchen, leaving Tad and Billy alone. Billy pours himself a glass of ginger ale.)

BILLY: Is it time . . . ?
TAD: You nervous?

(Billy shakes his head.)

I think about . . . When you come back? For good? I want to kiss you. Don't say anything. Just . . . sit somewhere, you know, out of, away, just . . . your head in my lap and . . . Just sit. Okay? And . . . Hold your face in my hands. I've gotta . . . I think about it. I've gotta kiss you. *(Pause)* I've gotta kiss you.
BILLY: We'll / s[ee]—
TAD: No, say yes. You want it. You have.
BILLY: It's just you haven't had sex.
TAD: No, it's you. I'm gonna freeze to death in here if I don't kiss you. Say yes. Come on. Say yes.

(Billy covers his face, sits.)

It's okay.

BILLY: No!

TAD: I know you're straight.

BILLY: No. No, I'm not. But it's just . . . to be even seen by anybody.

TAD: Yes!

BILLY: You're married to my sister.

TAD: She's not gonna know. I love you both. She's not. You want it. You want to kiss me.

(Billy glances to see that they are alone, then he kisses Tad. They move apart as Marianne returns, followed by Karen and Dolores. Marianne senses something between Tad and Billy.)

(Sotto voce to Billy) After the service we'll take a walk.

(Marianne pours the rest of her drink into Karen's.)

KAREN: I thought you said watch.

MARIANNE: Changed my mind.

(Marianne approaches Tad and Billy.)

TAD *(Continues softly)*: Just go somewhere. Just us. Say yes.

MARIANNE: Ready?

TAD: Yes. Say yes.

BILLY: No.

TAD: Yes!

MARIANNE: Are you okay?

BILLY: No. *(Directly to Tad)* No.

MARIANNE: What's . . . ?

(Short pause.)

BILLY *("Let's start the service."):* Come on.

(Dolores picks up a spoon; she taps a glass, speaking to the unseen mourners:)

DOLORES: Could we . . . ? Could we have everyone's—?

(Billy takes the glass and spoon from Dolores. He indicates that she should step back.)

BILLY: Welcome, everybody. My family and I thank you all for being here. Anyone who wants to say anything will get a chance. This is a celebration. *(Short pause)* Marianne?

(Marianne steps forward; Billy steps back.)

MARIANNE: As most of you prob'ly know, Dad's favorite band was the Grateful Dead. So— And in thinking about today, the thing that kept coming to us, what to say, or would be worthy . . . Dad would say to us when something crummy would happen: "Where's the gift, what's the gift? Look for the gift." We thought he was nuts, well—he was nuts— But . . . to look for the gift. You're all here, we're together. Yeah, because he's gone, and still we're grateful.

(Marianne steps back. She looks at Billy: "Your turn." Billy moves center, but is intercepted by Karen who has also moved forward; Billy gives her the spotlight, retreating slightly.)

KAREN: I think I'm in some kind of trance state still, but . . . Oh. Since we're . . . holding up evidence, I don't know, for the Defense. Or Prosecution, I have no clue what I'm saying.

(She produces a public service brochure.)

This came in the mail today. Did, I don't know how many of you have seen this: It's a brochure for public safety, paid for by . . . us, I suppose, and printed for us. For those who wish to acquire iodine to prevent their bodies from absorbing too much radiation in the event of an accident at Indian Point. The nuclear power plant that's three and a half miles from here. A fully functioning and perfectly visible, if . . . they say if it explodes, something like fourteen million people could die. You could not make this up. I thought, This is a movie, something people would go to see where millions of people are washed away in a . . . wave. Oh, and you can't take the iodine if you're allergic to shellfish, so . . . *(Pause)* We're in a relay race. People. You take the baton. You take the baton.

(Billy and Marianne have moved in toward Karen, concerned that she is going to embarrass herself.)

I thought my daughter was going to say, about the Grateful Dead. *(Touches herself)* Grateful. *(Indicates the casket)* Dead. Not really. But I'm glad she didn't. That's enough! No, I'm done! I'm done!

(The baby starts to fuss.)

BILLY: You sure?
MARIANNE: That was beautiful.
KAREN: Done.

(Tad quiets the baby. Billy produces a folded piece of yellow, lined paper.)

BILLY: This was in Dad's—we found this in his things. He would write these out; I walked in on him once by mistake and saw him on his knees, head bowed, reading. *(Reads)* "God. Love, guide and protect those who would seem to harm me . . . To the Iraqi—citizen, soldier and insurgent—grant peace of mind, long life, prosperity; anything and everything I would wish for myself, give to him. Or her. A sense of purpose, of fit. May he wake up to life's bounty and know he does your bidding. Give him passion, delight, worthy challenges, wisdom and surprise. May he never come to make or inhabit a land so indecent as the one that lives in me. May he bask . . . " You know he had his thesaurus for that. "May he bask in your perfection and be complete in all ways, to your design. Amen."

DOLORES: Amen.

BILLY *(Staring at Dolores)*: Not bad. Kind of amazing, actually.

KAREN: That's the man I remember. Sorry.

BILLY: No.

KAREN: That's who he used to be. That's who's died.

(She points to the casket.)

Now I'm done.

(Dolores bursts into tears, sinks into a chair.)

DOLORES: I'm sorry. I'm sorry. I'm sorry. I'm so sorry! I'm sorry . . .

(At last, Billy moves to Dolores and comforts her; she buries her face against his chest. Finally, Billy looks toward Karen and Marianne: It's okay. Then, to Tad:)

BILLY: Go ahead.

(Tad steps forward.)

TAD: This is uhhhh "Slane, Be Thou My Vision." It's an Irish, I think it's originally in Gaelic—

(Tad hands the baby over to Marianne.)

Anyway, cross your fingers.

(The baby is crying.)

Don't you love . . . I mean . . . that the baby has no idea what we're going through . . . I mean, he's oblivious. That's the idea: We get another chance, it doesn't matter, they don't just, I mean, they don't just see us as heroes, we get a chance to see ourselves, to step up, you know . . . to . . . I mean, who wouldn't love them, if just for that. We step up . . . Love that.

(Beat. He sings:)

> Be thou my vision, O Lord of my heart.
> Naught be all else to me save that thou art.
> Thou my best thought by day or by night,
> Waking or sleeping thy presence my light.

(The others join in:)

ALL:

> Be thou my wisdom, thou my true word,
> I ever with thee, thou with me, Lord,
> Thou my great Father, I thy true Son,
> Thou in me dwelling, and I with thee one.

END OF PLAY

Craig Lucas's plays include *Missing Persons*, *Blue Window*, *Reckless*, *Prelude to a Kiss*, *God's Heart*, *The Dying Gaul*, *Stranger*, *Small Tragedy* and *The Singing Forest*. He wrote the book for *The Light in the Piazza*, music and lyrics by Adam Guettel; the musical play *Three Postcards*, music and lyrics by Craig Carnelia; the libretto for the opera *Orpheus in Love*, music by Gerald Busby; and he has recently completed the libretto for *Two Boys*, an opera with composer Nico Muhly, commissioned by the Metropolitan Opera and scheduled to premiere there in a co-production with the English National Opera. His new English adaptations include Brecht's *Galileo*, Chekhov's *Three Sisters* and *Uncle Vanya*, and Strindberg's *Miss Julie*. His screenplays include *Longtime Companion* (Sundance Audience Award), *The Secret Lives of Dentists* (New York Film Critics Circle Best Screenplay Award), *Prelude to a Kiss*, *Reckless* and *The Dying Gaul*, which he also directed. He directed Harry Kondoleon's plays *Saved or Destroyed* at the Rattlestick Playwrights Theater (Obie Award for Best Director) and *Play Yourself* at the New York Theatre Workshop, as well as his own play *This Thing of Darkness* (co-authored with David Schulner) at the Atlantic Theater Company. He also directed the film *Birds of America*. Twice nominated for a Tony (*Prelude to a Kiss* and *The Light in the Piazza*), three times for the Drama Desk (*Prelude to a Kiss*, *Missing Persons* and *Reckless*), he has won the Los Angeles Drama Critics Award (*Blue Window*), the Steinberg/American Theater Critics Award for Best American Play (*The Singing Forest*), the Hull-Warriner Award (*The Light in the Piazza*), the LAMBDA Literary Award (for his anthology *What I Meant Was*), the Flora Roberts Award, the Academy Award in Literature from the American Academy of Arts and Letters, the Laura Pels/PEN Mid-Career Achievement Award and the Joan Cullman Award; he has twice won the Obie Award for Best Play (*Prelude to a Kiss* and *Small Tragedy*).